The Olympic Games

Contents

**Written by
John Foster**

Collins

What are the Olympic Games?

The Olympic Games are the world's largest sporting event. Top sports stars from about 200 different countries take part. They compete against each other in more than 300 different events.

the opening ceremony of the 2008 Beijing Olympics

It's a great honour to represent your country at the Olympic Games. Many sports stars see winning an Olympic gold medal as the greatest achievement of their sporting career.

Julie Pomagalski of France competes in the women's snowboard race at the 2006 Turin Olympics.

Dimitry Klokov of Russia at the Beijing Olympics

Christine Ohuruogu of Great Britain wins the women's 400 metres at the Beijing Olympics.

3

The ancient Olympic Games

The ancient Olympic Games were held at Olympia in Greece. The Games were part of a religious festival in honour of Zeus, the king of the ancient Greek gods. The first Games took place in 776 BC. There was only one event, a sprint of about 192 metres, called "the stadion". Over the years, more events were added.

Athens

Olympia

GREECE

The stadion sprint race: athletes in the ancient Olympic Games competed in the nude.

Winners were given a crown made of olive branches from a **sacred** tree near the temple of Zeus.

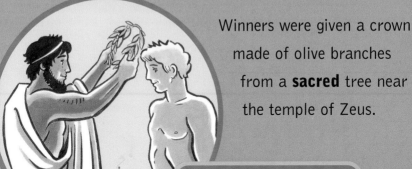

The winner was crowned with olive leaves.

The ancient Olympics were held every four years for more than 1,100 years, until they were banned by the Roman Emperor, Theodosius, in 393 AD.

The ancient Games were for men and boys only and lasted for five days.

Day 1

Races for young athletes aged between 12 and 18.

Day 2

Morning: horse and chariot races.
Afternoon: the pentathlon, which consisted of five events: **discus** throwing, **javelin** throwing, running, long jump and wrestling.

Day 3

Races, including the long-distance race and the sprint.

the chariot race

Boxing and wrestling, including a violent event called the pankration, in which there were no rules except that biting was not allowed. The Games finished with a race that involved men running while carrying armour and a shield.

athletes competing in the final race of the Games

Day 5

A day of celebration, when prizes were awarded, followed by a feast.

How did the modern Olympics begin?

The first modern Olympic Games were held in Athens, the capital of Greece, in 1896. There were 245 competitors from 14 countries, who took part in 43 events.

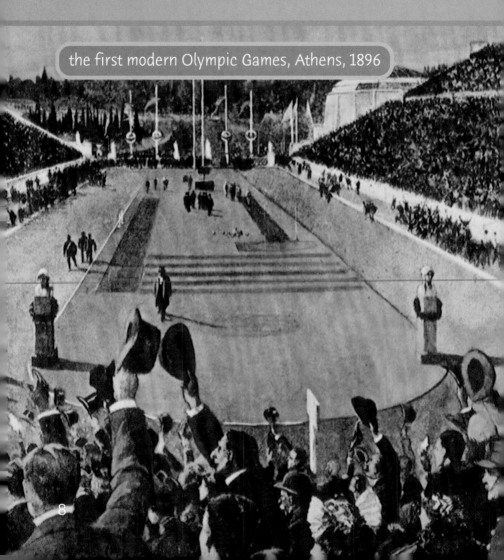

the first modern Olympic Games, Athens, 1896

A Frenchman named Baron Pierre de Coubertin had the idea to hold an international Olympic Games. He designed the Olympic flag, which has five interlocking rings of different colours. The rings represent the continents of Africa, the Americas, Asia, Australia and Europe, linking their peoples together in friendship.

Baron Pierre de Coubertin

the Olympic flag

Where are the Olympic Games held?

The Olympic Games are held every four years in different cities around the world. Members of the International Olympic Committee (IOC) vote to decide which city will host the Games.

There are always many countries competing to hold the Olympic Games as they attract thousands of tourists.

The tourists who come to see the events will spend money on transport, hotels and in restaurants. Hosting the Olympic Games also makes people very proud that their country has been chosen.

athletics taking place in the Olympic Stadium, Sydney, Australia, 2000

The timeline shows the cities that have held the Olympic Games since the end of the Second World War.

1948	London, Great Britain
1952	Helsinki, Finland
1956	Melbourne, Australia
1960	Rome, Italy
1964	Tokyo, Japan
1968	Mexico City, Mexico
1972	Munich, West Germany
1976	Montreal, Canada
1980	Moscow, USSR
1984	Los Angeles, USA
1988	Seoul, South Korea
1992	Barcelona, Spain
1996	Atlanta, USA
2000	Sydney, Australia
2004	Athens, Greece
2008	Beijing, China

the opening ceremony of the 1964 Tokyo Olympics

An image of the famous Russian revolutionary Lenin was created as part of the opening ceremony of the 1980 Moscow Olympics.

11

Staging the Olympics

It costs a huge amount of money for a country to stage the Olympic Games. Work begins many years before the Games. A new **stadium** usually has to be built, and new roads, railway lines and train stations, so that people can reach it. Suitable places have to be chosen for events such as rowing and cycling. An Olympic village has to be constructed for the 12,000 athletes to stay in during the Games.

the National Aquatics Centre

the Beijing Olympic Village

Some of the money for staging the Games comes from television companies, who buy the rights to show the Games on TV around the world. More money comes from companies that pay to be official **sponsors** of the Games. But a great amount of money still has to be found by the people of the country which hosts the Games.

the Beijing National Stadium, also known as the "Bird's Nest"

The torch relay

During the ancient Olympics a sacred flame burnt at the altar of Zeus. The first modern Games at which an Olympic flame burnt were those held in Amsterdam in 1928.

Nowadays, several months before the start of the Games, a torch is lit at Olympia by reflecting the Sun's rays from a mirror. Different runners then carry the torch around the world, visiting major cities on the way.

Hundreds of runners each carry the torch for part of the journey, before passing it to the next runner.

The ancient flame was lit in front of the Temple of Hera by a priestess.

Finally, the torch is carried into the Olympic stadium and used to light a flame that burns throughout the Games. The first torch **relay** took place before the 1936 Olympics in Berlin, Germany.

A torch bearer carries the Olympic flame before the 1936 Berlin Olympics.

The opening ceremony

The opening **ceremony** is a spectacular event. During the ceremony, there is a parade of athletes from every nation taking part and the Olympic flag is raised.

The opening ceremony often includes singing, dancing, music and fantastic firework displays. The Olympic flame is lit and doves are then released as symbols of peace.

the opening ceremony
of the Beijing Olympics

17

Olympic sports

Athletics

In the modern Olympic Games there are events in 28 different sports.

Athletics events are divided into track events and field events. On the track, runners compete over distances from 100 metres to 10,000 metres. There are also sprint races over hurdles and a 3,000-metre steeplechase in which competitors have to jump over hurdles and water jumps.

the men's 3,000-metre steeplechase final at the Beijing Olympics

Did you know?

An athlete from Kenya won the gold medal for the 3,000-metre steeplechase in every Olympics that Kenya competed in from 1968 to 2008.

The longest race is the marathon, which is 42 kilometres in length. It's run on roads surrounding the stadium and finishes with a lap of the stadium.

At the end of the 1908 Olympic marathon Dorando Pietri of Italy entered the stadium first, but then collapsed five times on the final lap. Officials helped him to stagger over the line, but he was disqualified for receiving help.

Dorando Pietri finishing the marathon in the 1908 London Olympics

19

Field events are divided into two types: throwing events such as the javelin and the hammer, and jumping events such as the high jump and pole vault.

Yipsi Moreno of Cuba throwing the hammer in the Beijing finals

Did you know?

In 1972, Ulrike Meyfarth from Germany became the youngest winner of an individual athletics gold medal, when she won the high jump at the age of 16.

The decathlon and heptathlon

Men take part in the decathlon, which consists of ten athletics events. Women take part in the heptathlon, which consists of seven athletics events. Points are awarded for a competitor's performance in each event and the winner is regarded as the best all-round athlete.

Events include:

- races over various distances
- jumping events
- throwing events.

Liudmyla Blonska of Ukraine throws the javelin at the Beijing Olympics.

Great Britain's Dean Macey doing the long jump at the Sydney Olympics

Aquatic sports

Swimming, diving and **water polo** are called **aquatic sports**, because they take place in water.

In **synchronised** swimming, pairs or teams of eight have to perform a routine to music. The swimmers have to do all their movements at exactly the same time.

the USA's synchronised swimming team at the Sydney Olympics

Did you know?

In 1896, swimming events were held in the sea and in 1900 they were held in the River Seine in Paris. The swimmers recorded fast times because they swam with the current!

Diving events involve jumping from a 10-metre high platform or a 3-metre high springboard.

Rowing, canoeing, kayaking and sailing

In rowing events, rowers compete over a 2,000-metre course.

Did you know?

Between 1984 and 2000 Sir Steve Redgrave of Great Britain became the only rower to win five gold medals at five different Olympics.

There are flat-water, canoe and kayak races and fast-water events in rapid water, in which competitors have to go through a number of gates in the fastest time.

Did you know?

In 2004, Birgit Fischer, a German canoeist aged 42, became the first woman in any sport to win gold medals at six different Olympic Games.

Did you know?

Ben Ainslie was just 19 when he won a silver medal in sailing for Great Britain in the 1996 Atlanta Olympics. He went on to win gold medals in 2000, 2004 and 2008. Ben is superstitious and always eats a Chinese meal before an Olympic race.

Did you know?

In 1988, Lawrence Lemieux of Canada was coming second in a yachting race, when he stopped to help another sailor whose boat had sunk. He finished 21st, but was later awarded a special medal.

Equestrian sports

Events which involve horses and riders are called **equestrian** sports.

There are three different types of event:

- In **dressage**, the horses have to perform a set of movements and marks are awarded for accuracy, obedience and performance.
- In show-jumping, competitors have to jump over obstacles as fast as possible without knocking any down.
- Three-day eventing consists of dressage and show-jumping and a test of stamina, which includes a cross-country course.

Did you know?

Denmark's Lis Hartel won a silver medal for dressage in the 1952 Helsinki Olympics, despite having to be lifted on and off her horse, because she had polio as a child and her legs were paralysed below the knees.

Taizo Sugitani of Japan competing on his horse "California" in the show-jumping event at the Beijing Olympics

Ball sports

Football is one of the many ball sports in the Olympic Games, along with others such as basketball, hockey, tennis and table tennis. At the first modern Games in 1896, the football event was cancelled, because not enough people were interested in it! For the 2008 Games there were 16 men's teams and 12 women's.

Spain plays South Korea in a hockey match at the Beijing Olympics.

Argentina plays Lithuania in a basketball match at the Beijing Olympics.

Did you know?

In the 2004 football tournament, Iraq produced a shock result by beating Portugal, whose team included Cristiano Ronaldo!

Combat sports

Combat sports include boxing, wrestling, judo and tae kwon do.

An Olympic boxing match consists of four two-minute rounds. Time limits for wrestling were introduced in 1924. In the 1912 Olympics one fight lasted for 11 hours and 40 minutes!

Did you know?

In 1964, Joe Frazier from the USA won the heavyweight boxing final, despite having a broken hand.

In judo, competitors wrestle and grapple each other in an attempt to throw and hold their opponent so as to score points. In tae kwon do, competitors score points by kicking and punching. Points are taken off for illegal hits, such as blows below the waist.

Dongmin Cha of Korea fights Alexandros Nikolaidis of Greece for a gold medal in tae kwon do at the Beijing Olympics.

Other Olympic sports

In archery, competitors aim at a target 70 metres away. The centre of the target is known as the bull's-eye and has a diameter of only 12.2 centimetres.

Cycling is divided into track racing, road racing, mountain biking and BMX racing. A track bicycle costs at least £10,000. It has fixed wheels and no gears and is controlled by how hard the rider presses down on the pedals.

Jason Kenny and Chris Hoy of Great Britain during the men's sprint final at the Beijing Olympics

In gymnastics, competitors perform exercises on floor mats and pieces of apparatus such as the parallel bars. Points are awarded out of ten.

At the 1976 Montreal Olympics, Romanian teenager Nadia Comaňeci was given seven perfect ten scores.

Nadia Comaňeci wins a gold medal on the balance beam at the Moscow Olympics.

Did you know?

Between 1956 and 1964, the Russian gymnast Larissa Latynina won a record 18 medals, including nine gold medals.

The Paralympic Games

The Paralympics, which are Olympic Games for people with disabilities, take place every four years in the same city as the Olympic Games. The first official Paralympics took place in Rome in 1960.

Athletes are divided into six different groups according to their disability. For example, there are separate events for athletes who are blind or cannot see very well and for athletes who have lost a limb.

Did you know?

Eleanor Simmonds, who has a form of dwarfism, became Britain's youngest individual gold medallist at the age of 13 at the 2008 Beijing Paralympics.

There are competitions in about 20 different sports ranging from athletics and archery to wheelchair basketball.

Australia plays Japan in a wheelchair basketball match at the Beijing Paralympics.

Did you know?

During her sporting career, wheelchair-racer Dame Tanni Grey-Thompson of Great Britain won 16 medals. Eleven were gold medals!

Today, artificial limbs are made from very light metals so athletes are able to run much faster than before.

Did you know?

Oscar Pistorius from South Africa won the 100-, 200- and 400-metre sprints at the Beijing Paralympics. He has two artificial lower legs.

The Winter Olympic Games

The Winter Olympics are held two years after the Summer Olympics. They consist of snow sports and ice sports, so they have to be held in countries where there are mountains covered in snow such as France, USA, Canada or Italy. The Winter Paralympic Games are held in the same city and involve five sporting events.

Snow sports

Snow sports include skiing, ski jumping and snowboarding.

Gregory Baxter of Canada on the ski jumping slope at the Turin Olympics

Downhill ski races are held on steep slopes and racers reach speeds of more than 75 miles an hour. Ski jumpers ski down a ramp, reaching speeds of up to 38 miles an hour at take off. The winner is the person who jumps the furthest. It can be a very dangerous event.

Switzerland's Daniel Albrecht loses control at the Turin Olympics.

Ice sports

Ice sports include ice hockey, skating and races on sledges.

In bobsleigh races, teams of two or four people hurtle down tracks of ice at speeds of up to 94 miles per hour.

Did you know?

The bobsleigh is so-named because of the way crews originally bobbed back and forth to increase their speed at the start.

In luge races, sledders lie back on a sledge called a luge to make it go as fast as possible.

Chris and Mike Moffat of Canada in the men's luge double final at the Turin Olympics

Skaters compete in speed skating and figure skating events, in which skaters perform routines, including dances and lifts.

women's short track speed skating, 2002 Salt Lake City Olympics

Olympic medals

At the 1896 Olympics the winners were presented with an olive branch, a certificate and a silver medal. The 1904 Olympics were the first at which there was a gold medal for first place, a silver medal for second place and a bronze medal for third place.

Today, the medals are presented shortly after each event. At the medal ceremony, the three medallists stand on a **podium**. The national flags of their countries are raised and the **national anthem** of the winner's country is played.

Italy, Russia and Austria celebrate their medal wins for cross-country skiing at the Turin Olympics.

Going for glory – training for the Olympic Games

If you want to become an Olympic athlete, you not only need to be talented, you also have to work hard. Athletes have to be very disciplined. Most athletes train at least five times a week.

But it's a great thrill if you're chosen to represent your country. It's an even greater thrill if you win a medal!

Badminton champion Lin Dan of China shows off his gold medal at the Beijing Olympics.

Glossary

aquatic sports	sports that are performed in or on water
ceremony	a formal celebration of an event
discus	a circular object with a heavy middle
dressage	the art of a horse performing a set of movements under instruction from its rider
equestrian	something that is to do with horses or horse riding
javelin	a long, pointed spear
national anthem	a special song sung by a nation at public events
podium	a small, raised platform
relay	a team of people, taking over a task one after another
sacred	something with a special religious meaning
sponsors	people who support an event, usually with money
stadium	a sports arena with raised rows of seats for people to sit in
synchronised	taking place at precisely the same time
water polo	a game played in water by two teams of seven swimmers, with the aim of scoring goals by throwing a ball

Index

EVENTS IN THE ANCIENT, 1896 AND 2008 OLYMPICS

Ancient Olympics	1896 Athens Olympics
	SWIMMING
LONG-DISTANCE RUNNING	ATHLETICS
RUNNING CARRYING ARMOUR AND A SHIELD	ATHLETICS
SPRINTING	ATHLETICS
BOXING	
	CYCLING
CHARIOT RACING	
HORSE RACING	
	FENCING
	GYMNASTICS
PENTATHLON	
	SHOOTING
	TENNIS
	WEIGHTLIFTING
WRESTLING	WRESTLING

2008 Beijing Olympics

AQUATICS
ARCHERY
ATHLETICS
ATHLETICS

ATHLETICS
BADMINTON
BASEBALL
BASKETBALL
BOXING
CANOEING
CYCLING
EQUESTRIAN
EQUESTRIAN
FENCING
FIELD HOCKEY
FOOTBALL
GYMNASTICS
HANDBALL
JUDO
MODERN PENTATHLON
ROWING
SAILING
SHOOTING
SOFTBALL
TABLE TENNIS
TAE KWON DO
TENNIS
TRIATHLON
VOLLEYBALL
WEIGHTLIFTING
WRESTLING

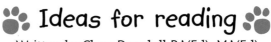 Ideas for reading

Written by Clare Dowdall BA(Ed), MA(Ed)
Lecturer and Primary Literacy Consultant

Learning objectives: identify and make notes of the main points of the main sections of text; identify how different texts are organised; use talk to organise roles and action

Curriculum links: Citizenship: Living in a diverse world; Geography: Connecting ourselves to the world

Interest words: aquatic, ceremony, discus, dressage, equestrian, javelin, podium, relay, sacred, steeplechase, synchronised

Resources: ICT, whiteboards

Getting started

This book can be read over two or more guided reading sessions.

- Ask children to recall any experiences of watching the Olympic Games.

- Collect information about the Olympic Games on a whiteboard using the following headings: What are the Olympic Games? Where are the Olympic Games held? Who participates in the Olympic Games?

- Look at the front and back covers together and read the blurb to the children. Discuss what is happening in the pictures (*men's sprint, medal ceremony*).

Reading and responding

- Read pp2–3 to the children. Model how to make a note of the main points from reading by recounting three important facts, e.g. *it is the largest sporting event in the world, with 200 countries competing in 300 events.*

- In pairs, ask children to read pp4–7 to learn about the ancient Olympic Games.

- Ask pairs to play an *important facts game*, where they take turns to recall important facts from reading. The winner is the child who recalls the most facts, or the team with the most facts.